The Shepherd's Calendar

JOHN CLARE

A Phoenix Paperback

Selected Poems by John Clare first published by J. M. Dent in 1965

This abridged edition first published in 1996 by Phoenix
a division of Orion Books Ltd
Orion House, 5 Upper St Martin's Lane, London WC2H 9EA

Copyright © Orion Books Ltd 1996

Cover illustration: *Sunset*, by John Linnell, Fine Art Photographic Library

ISBN 1 85799 660 7

Typeset by Deltatype Ltd, Ellesmere Port, Cheshire
Printed in Great Britain by
Clays Ltd, St Ives plc

CONTENTS

From *The Shepherd's Calendar*
January

I

Withering and keen the winter comes,
While Comfort flies to close-shut rooms,
And sees the snow in feathers pass
Winnowing by the window-glass;
Whilst unfelt tempests howl and beat
Above his head in chimney-seat.

Now, musing o'er the changing scene,
Farmers behind the tavern-screen
Collect; with elbow idly press'd
On hob, reclines the corner's guest,
Reading the news, to mark again
The bankrupt lists, or price of grain;
Or old Moore's annual prophecies
Of flooded fields and clouded skies;
Whose Almanac's thumb'd pages swarm
With frost and snow, and many a storm,
And wisdom, gossip'd from the stars,
Of politics and bloody wars.
He shakes his head, and still proceeds,
Nor doubts the truth of what he reads:

All wonders are with faith supplied –
Bible, at once, and weather-guide.
Puffing the while his red-tipt pipe,
He dreams o'er troubles nearly ripe;
Yet, not quite lost in profit's way,
He'll turn to next year's harvest-day,
And, winter's leisure to regale,
Hope better times, and sip his ale.

The schoolboy still, with dithering joys,
In pastime leisure hours employs,
And, be the weather as it may,
Is never at a loss for play:
Making rude forms of various names,
Snow-men, or aught his fancy frames;
Till, numb'd and shivering, he resorts
To brisker games and warmer sports –
Kicking, with many a flying bound,
The football o'er the frozen ground,
Or seeking bright glib ice, to play
And slide the wintry hours away,
As quick and smooth as shadows run,
When clouds in autumn pass the sun.
Some, hurrying rambles eager take
To skate upon the meadow lake,
Scaring the snipe from her retreat,
From shelving bank's unfrozen seat,
Or running brook, where icy spars,

Which the pale sunlight specks with stars,
Shoot crizzling o'er the restless tide,
To many a likeness petrified.
The moor-hen, too, with fear opprest,
Starts from her reedy shelter'd rest,
As skating by, with curving springs,
And arms outspread like heron's wings,
They race away, for pleasure's sake,
With hunter's speed along the lake.

Blackening through the evening sky,
In clouds the starnels daily fly
To Whittlesea's reed-wooded mere,
And osier holts by rivers near;
Whilst many a mingled swarthy crowd –
Rook, crow, and jackdaw – noising loud,
Fly to and fro to dreary fen,
Dull winter's weary flight again;
They flop on heavy wings away
As soon as morning wakens grey,
And, when the sun sets round and red,
Return to naked woods to bed.
Wood pigeons too in flocks appear,
By hunger tamed from timid fear;
They mid the sheep unstartled steal
And share with them a scanty meal,
Picking the green leaves want bestows
Of turnips sprouting thro' the snows.

The sun is creeping out of sight
Behind the woods – whilst running night
Hastens to shut the day's dull eye,
And grizzle o'er the chilly sky,
Dark, deep and thick, by day forsook,
As cottage chimney's sooty nook.
Now maidens, fresh as summer roses,
Journeying from the distant closes,
Haste home with yokes and swinging pail;
The thresher, too, sets by his flail,
And leaves the mice at peace again
To fill their holes with stolen grain;
Whilst owlets, glad his toils are o'er,
Swoop by him as he shuts the door.

Bearing his hook beneath his arm,
The shepherd seeks the cottage warm;
And, weary in the cold to roam,
Scenting the track that leads him home,
His dog goes swifter o'er the mead,
Barking to urge his master's speed;
Then turns, and looks him in the face,
And trots before with mending pace,
Till, out of whistle from the swain,
He sits him down and barks again,
Anxious to greet the open'd door,
And meet the cottage fire once more.

The robin, that with nimble eye
Glegs round a danger to espy,
Now pops from out the open door
From crumbs half left upon the floor,
Nor wipes his bill on perching chair,
Nor stays to clean a feather there,
Scared at the cat that slinketh in
A chance from evening's glooms to win,
To jump on chairs or tables high,
Seeking what plunder may supply,
The children's littered scraps to thieve
Or aught that negligence may leave,
Creeping, where housewives cease to watch
Or diary doors are off the latch,
On cheese or butter to regale
Or new milk reeking in the pail.
The hedger now in leather coat,
From woodland wild and fields remote,
After a journey far and slow,
Knocks from his shoes the caking snow
And opes the welcome creaking door,
Throwing his faggot on the floor;
And at his listening wife's desire
To eke afresh the blazing fire
With sharp bill cuts the hazel bands,
Then sits him down to warm his hands
And tell in labour's happy way
His story of the passing day;

While as the warm blaze cracks and gleams
The supper reeks in savoury steams
Or kettle murmurs merrily
And tinkling cups are set for tea;
Thus doth the winter's dreary day
From morn to evening wear away.

2

The shutter closed, the lamp alight,
The faggot chopt and blazing bright –
The shepherd now, from labour free,
Dances his children on his knee;
While, underneath his master's seat,
The tired dog lies in slumbers sweet,
Starting and whimpering in his sleep,
Chasing still the straying sheep.
The cat's roll'd round in vacant chair,
Or leaping children's knees to lair,
Or purring on the warmer hearth,
Sweet chorus to the cricket's mirth.

The redcap, hanging overhead,
In cage of wire is perch'd abed;
Slumbering in his painted feathers,
Unconscious of the outdoor weathers;
Ev'n things without the cottage walls
Meet comfort as the evening falls,
As happy in the winter's dearth

As those around the blazing hearth.
The ass (frost-driven from the moor,
Where storms through naked bushes roar,
And not a leaf or sprig of green,
On ground or quaking bush, is seen,
Save grey-vein'd ivy's hardy pride,
Round old trees by the common side),
Litter'd with straw, now dozes warm,
Beneath his shed, from snow and storm:
The swine are fed and in the sty;
And fowls snug perch'd in hovel nigh,
With head in feathers safe asleep,
Where foxes cannot hope to creep,
And geese are gabbling in their dreams
Of litter'd corn and thawing streams.
The sparrow, too, a daily guest,
Is in the cottage eaves at rest;
· And robin small, and smaller wren,
Are in their warm holes safe agen
From falling snows, that winnow by
The hovels where they nightly lie,
And ague winds, that shake the tree
Where other birds are forc'd to be.

    The housewife, busy night and day,
Clears the supper-things away;
The jumping cat starts from her seat;
And stretching up on weary feet,

The dog wakes at the welcome tones
That call him up to pick the bones.

On corner walls, a glittering row,
Hang fire-irons – less for use than show,
With horse-shoe brighten'd, as a spell,
Witchcraft's evil powers to quell,
And warming-pan, reflecting bright
The cracking blaze's flickering light,
That hangs the corner wall to grace,
Nor oft is taken from its place:
There in its mirror, bright as gold,
The children peep, and straight behold
Their laughing faces, whilst they pass,
Gleam on the lid as plain as glass.

Supper removed, the mother sits,
And tells her tales by starts and fits.
Not willing to lose time or toil,
She knits or sews, and talks the while –
Something that may be warnings found
To the young listeners gaping round –
Of boys who in her early day
Stroll'd to the meadow-lake to play,
Where willows, o'er the bank inclined,
Shelter'd the water from the wind,
And left it scarcely crizzled o'er –
When one plopt in, to rise no more!
And how, upon a market-night,

8

When not a star bestow'd its light,
A farmer's shepherd, o'er his glass,
Forgot that he had woods to pass:
And having sold his master's sheep,
Was overta'en by darkness deep.
How, coming with his startled horse,
To where two roads a hollow cross,
Where, lone guide when a stranger strays,
A white post points four different ways,
Beside the woodride's lonely gate
A murdering robber lay in wait.
The frighten'd horse, with broken rein
Stood at the stable-door again;
But none came home to fill his rack,
Or take the saddle from his back:
The saddle – it was all he bore;
The man was seen alive no more!
In her young days, beside the wood,
The gibbet in his terror stood:
Though now decay'd, 'tis not forgot,
But dreaded as a haunted spot.

She from her memory oft repeats
Witches' dread powers and fairy feats:
How one has oft been known to prance
In cowcribs, like a coach, to France,
And ride on sheep-trays from the fold
A race-horse speed to Burton-hold,

To join the midnight mystery's rout,
Where witches meet the yews about:
And how, when met with unawares,
They turn at once to cats or hares,
And race along with hellish flight,
Now here, now there, now out of sight!
And how the other tiny things
Will leave their moonlight meadow-rings,
And, unperceiv'd, through key-holes creep,
When all around have sunk to sleep,
And crowd in cupboards as they please,
As thick as mites in rotten cheese,
To feast on what the cotter leaves –
Mice are not reckon'd greater thieves.
They take away, as well as eat,
And still the housewife's eye they cheat,
In spite of all the folks that swarm
In cottage small and larger farm;
They through each key-hole pop and pop,
Like wasps into a grocer's shop,
With all the things that they can win
From chance to put their plunder in;
As shells of walnuts, split in two
By crows, who with the kernels flew;
Or acorn-cups, by stock-doves pluck'd,
Or egg-shells by a cuckoo suck'd;
With broad leaves of the sycamore
They clothe their stolen dainties o'er,

And when in cellar they regale,
Bring hazel-nuts to hold their ale,
With bung-holes bor'd by squirrels well,
To get the kernel from the shell,
Or maggots a way out to win,
When all is gone that grew within;
And be the key-holes e'er so high,
Rush poles a ladder's help supply,
Where soft the climbers fearless tread
On spindles made of spiders' thread.
And foul, or fair, or dark the night,
Their wild-fire lamps are burning bright,
For which full many a daring crime
Is acted in the summer-time;
When glow-worm found in lanes remote
Is murder'd for its shining coat,
And put in flowers, that Nature weaves
With hollow shapes and silken leaves,
Such as the Canterbury bell,
Serving for lamp or lantern well;
Or, following with unwearied watch
The flight of one they cannot match,
As silence sliveth upon sleep,
Or thieves by dozing watch-dogs creep,
They steal from Jack-a-lantern's tails
A light, whose guidance never fails
To aid them in the darkest night
And guide their plundering steps aright,

Rattling away in printless tracks.
Some, housed on beetles' glossy backs,
Go whisking on – and others hie
As fast as loaded moths can fly:
Some urge, the morning cock to shun,
The hardest gallop mice can run,
In chariots, lolling at their ease,
Made of whate'er their fancies please;
Things that in childhood's memory dwell –
Scoop'd crow-pot-stone, or cockle-shell,
With wheels at hand of mallow seeds,
Where childish sport was stringing beads;
And thus equipp'd, they softly pass
Like shadows on the summer-grass,
And glide away in troops together
Just as the spring-wind drives a feather.
As light as happy dreams they creep,
Nor break the feeblest link of sleep:
A midgeon in their road abed,
Feels not the wheels run o'er his head,
But sleeps till sunrise calls him up,
Unconscious of the passing troop.

Thus dame the winter-night regales
With wonder's never-ceasing tales;
While in a corner, ill at ease,
Or crushing 'tween their father's knees,
The children – silent all the while –

And e'en repressed the laugh or smile –
Quake with the ague chills of fear,
And tremble though they love to hear,
Starting, while they the tales recall,
At their own shadows on the wall:
Till the old clock, that strikes unseen
Behind the picture-pasted screen
Where Eve and Adam still agree
To rob Life's fatal apple-tree,
Counts over bed-time's hour of rest,
And bids each be sleep's fearful guest.
She then her half-told tales will leave
To finish on tomorrow's eve.
The children steal away to bed,
And up the ladder softly tread,
Scarce daring – from their fearful joys –
To look behind or make a noise;
Nor speak a word, but still as sleep
They secret to their pillows creep,
And whisper o'er, in terror's way,
The prayers they dare no louder say,
Then hide their heads beneath the clothes,
And try in vain to seek repose;
While yet, to fancy's sleepless eye,
Witches on sheep-trays gallop by,
And fairies, like a rising spark,
Swarm twittering round them in the dark;

Till sleep creeps nigh to ease their cares,
And drops upon them unawares.

Oh, spirit of the days gone by –
Sweet childhood's fearful ecstasy!
The witching spells of winter nights,
Where are they fled with their delights?
When list'ning on the corner seat,
The winter evening's length to cheat,
I heard my mother's memory tell
Tales superstition loves so well:
Things said or sung a thousand times,
In simple prose or simpler rhymes.
Ah! where is page of poesy
So sweet as this was wont to be?
The magic wonders that deceived,
When fictions were as truths believed,
The fairy feats that once prevailed,
Told to delight, and never failed,
Where are they now, their fears and sighs,
And tears from founts of happy eyes?
I read in books, but find them not,
For poesy hath its youth forgot:
I hear them told to children still,
But fear numbs not my spirits chill:
I still see faces pale with dread,
While mine could laugh at what is said,
See tears imagined woes supply,
While mine with real cares are dry.

Where are they gone – the joys and fears,
The links, the life of other years?
I thought they twined around my heart
So close, that we could never part;
But Reason, like a winter's day,
Nipp'd childhood's visions all away,
Nor left behind one withering flower
To cherish in a lonely hour.
Memory may yet the themes repeat,
But childhood's heart hath ceased to beat
At tales, which reason's sterner lore
Turns like weak gossips from her door:
The Magic Fountain, where the head
Rose up, just as the startled maid
Was stooping from the weedy drink,
That did its half-hid mystery tell
To smooth its hair, and use it well;
Which, doing as it bade her do,
Turn'd to a king and lover too.
The tale of Cinderella, told
The winter through, and never old:
The pumpkin that, at her approach,
Was turn'd into a golden coach;
The rats that fairies' magic knew,
And instantly to horses grew;
The coachmen ready at her call,
To drive her to the Prince's ball,
With fur-changed jackets silver lined,

And tails hung 'neath their hats behind;
The golden glove, with fingers small,
She lost while dancing in the hall,
That was on every finger tried,
And fitted hers, and none beside,
When Cinderella, soon as seen,
Was woo'd and won, and made a Queen.
The Boy that did the Giant slay,
And gave his mother's cow away
For magic mask, that day or night,
When on, would keep him out of sight.
The running bean – not such as weaves
Round poles the height of cottage eaves,
But magic one – that travell'd high
Some steeple's journey up the sky,
And reach'd a giant's dwelling there,
A cloud-built castle in the air:
Where, venturing up the fearful height,
That serv'd him climbing half the night,
He search'd the giant's coffers o'er,
And never wanted riches more;
While, like a lion scenting food,
The giant roar'd, in hungry mood,
A storm of threats that might suffice
To freeze the hottest blood to ice.

I hear it now, nor dream of woes;
The storm is settled to repose.

Those fears are dead! What will not die
In fading Life's mortality?
Those truths have fled, and left behind
A real world and doubting mind.

May

Come, Queen of Months! in company
With all thy merry minstrelsy:
The restless cuckoo, absent long,
And twittering swallows' chimney-song;
With hedgerow crickets' notes, that run
From every bank that fronts the sun;
And swarthy bees, about the grass,
That stop with every bloom they pass,
And every minute, every hour,
Keep teasing weeds that wear a flower;
And toil, and childhood's humming joys,
For there is music in the noise
When village children, wild for sport,
In school-time's leisure, ever short,
Alternate catch the bounding ball,
Or run along the churchyard wall,
Capp'd with rude figured slabs, whose claims
In time's bad memory have no names,
Or race around the nooky church,
Or raise loud echoes in the porch,

Throw pebbles o'er the weathercock,
Viewing with jealous eyes the clock,
Or leap o'er grave-stones' leaning heights,
Uncheck'd by melancholy sights,
Though green grass swells in many a heap
Where kin, and friends, and parents sleep.
They think not, in their jovial cry,
The time will come when they shall lie
As lowly and as still as they,
While other boys above them play,
Heedless, as they are now, to know
The unconscious dust that lies below.

The driving boy, beside his team,
Of May-month's beauty now will dream,
And cock his hat, and turn his eye
On flower, and tree, and deepening sky;
And oft burst loud in fits of song,
And whistle as he reels along,
Cracking his whip in starts of joy –
A happy, dirty, driving boy.
The youth, who leaves his corner stool
Betimes for neighbouring village-school,
Where, as a mark to guide him right,
The church spire's all the way in sight,
With cheerings from his parents given,
Beneath the joyous smiles of heaven

Saunters, with many an idle stand,

With satchel swinging in his hand,
And gazes, as he passes by,
On everything that meets his eye.
Young lambs seem tempting him to play,
Dancing and bleating in his way;
With trembling tails and pointed ears
They follow him, and lose their fears;
He smiles upon their sunny faces,
And fain would join their happy races.
The birds, that sing on bush and tree,
Seem chirping for his company;
And all – in fancy's idle whim –
Seem keeping holiday, but him.
He lolls upon each resting stile,
To see the fields so sweetly smile,
To see the wheat grow green and long;
And lists the weeder's toiling song,
Or short note of the changing thrush
Above him in the whitethorn bush,
That o'er the leaning stile bends low
Its blooming mockery of snow.

Each hedge is cover'd thick with green;
And where the hedger late hath been,
Young tender shoots begin to grow
From out the mossy stumps below.
But woodmen still on spring intrude,
And thin the shadow's solitude;

With sharpen'd axes felling down
The oak-trees budding into brown,
Which, as they crash upon the ground,
A crowd of labourers gather round.
These, mixing 'mong the shadows dark,
Rip off the crackling, staining bark,
Depriving yearly, when they come,
The green woodpecker of his home,
Who early in the spring began,
Far from the sight of troubling man,
To bore his round holes in each tree
In fancy's sweet security;
Now, startled by the woodman's noise,
He wakes from all his dreary joys.
The blue-bells too, that thickly bloom
Where man was never known to come;
And stooping lilies of the valley,
That love with shades and dews to dally,
And bending droop on slender threads,
With broad hood-leaves above their heads,
Like white-robed maids, in summer hours,
Beneath umbrellas shunning showers;
These, from the bark-men's crushing treads,
Oft perish in their blooming beds.
Stripp'd of its boughs and bark, in white
The trunk shines in the mellow light
Beneath the green surviving trees,
That wave above it in the breeze,

And, waking whispers, slowly bend,
As if they mourn'd their fallen friend.

Each morning, now, the weeders meet
To cut the thistle from the wheat,
And ruin, in the sunny hours,
Full many a wild weed with its flowers;
Corn-poppies, that in crimson dwell,
Call'd 'headaches,' from their sickly smell;
And charlocks, yellow as the sun,
That o'er the May-fields quickly run;
And 'iron-weed,' content to share
The meanest spot that spring can spare –
E'en roads, where danger hourly comes,
Are not without its purple blooms,
Whose leaves, with threat'ning thistles round
Thick set, that have no strength to wound,
Shrink into childhood's eager hold
Like hair; and, with its eye of gold
And scarlet-starry points of flowers,
Pimpernel, dreading nights and showers,
Oft call'd 'the shepherd's weather-glass,'
That sleeps till suns have dried the grass,
Then wakes, and spreads its creeping bloom
Till clouds with threatening shadows come –
Then close it shuts to sleep again:
Which weeders see, and talk of rain;
And boys, that mark them shut so soon,

Call them 'John-go-to-bed-at-noon.'
And fumitory too – a name
That superstition holds to fame –
Whose red and purple mottled flowers
Are cropp'd by maids in weeding hours,
To boil in water, milk, and whey,
For washes on a holiday,
To make their beauty fair and sleek,
And scare the tan from summer's cheek:
And simple small 'forget-me-not,'
Eyed with a pin's-head yellow spot
I' the middle of its tender blue,
That gains from poets notice due:
These flowers, that toil by crowds destroys,
Robbing them of their lowly joys,
Had met the May with hopes as sweet
As those her suns in gardens meet;
And oft the dame will feel inclined,
As childhood's memory comes to mind,
To turn her hook away, and spare
The blooms it loved to gather there.
– Now young girls whisper things of love,
And from the old dames' hearing move;
Oft making 'love-knots' in the shade,
Of blue-green oat or wheaten blade;
Or, trying simple charms and spells
Which rural superstition tells,
They pull the little blossom threads

From out the knotweed's button heads,
And put the husk, with many a smile,
In their white bosoms for a while –
Then, if they guess aright the swain
Their loves' sweet fancies try to gain,
'Tis said, that ere it lies an hour,
'Twill blossom with a second flower,
And from their bosom's handkerchief
Bloom as it ne'er had lost a leaf.
– But signs appear that token wet,
While they are 'neath the bushes met;
The girls are glad with hopes of play,
And harp upon the holiday:
A high blue bird is seen to swim
Along the wheat, when skies grow dim
With clouds; slow as the gales of spring
In motion, with dark-shadow'd wing
Beneath the coming storm he sails:
And lonely chirp the wheat-hid quails,
That come to live with spring again,
But leave when summer browns the grain;
They start the young girls' joys afloat,
With 'wet my foot' – their yearly note:
So fancy doth the sound explain,
And oft it proves a sign of rain!

The thresher, dull as winter days,
And lost to all that spring displays,

Still mid his barn-dust forced to stand,
Swings round his flail with weary hand;
While o'er his head shades thickly creep,
That hide the blinking owl asleep,
And bats, in cobweb-corners bred,
Sharing till night their murky bed.
The sunshine trickles on the floor
Through ev'ry crevice of the door:
This makes his barn, where shadows dwell,
As irksome as a prisoner's cell;
And, whilst he seeks his daily meal,
As schoolboys from their task will steal,
So will he stand with fond delay
To see the daisy in his way,
Or wild weeds flowering on the wall;
For these to memory still recall
The joys, the sports that come with spring –
The twirling top, the marble ring,
The jingling halfpence hustled up
At pitch-and-toss, the eager stoop
To pick up *heads*, the smuggled plays
'Neath hovels upon sabbath-days,
The sitting down, when school was o'er,
Upon the threshold of the door,
Picking from mallows, sport to please,
Each crumpled seed he call'd a cheese,
And hunting from the stack-yard sod
The stinking henbane's belted pod,

By youth's warm fancies sweetly led
To christen them his loaves of bread.
He sees, while rocking down the street
With weary hands and crimpling feet,
Young children at the self-same games,
And hears the self-same boyish names
Still floating on each happy tongue:
Touch'd with the simple scene so strong,
Tears almost start, and many a sigh
Regrets the happiness gone by;
Thus, in sweet Nature's holiday,
His heart is sad while all is gay.

How lovely now are lanes and balks,
For lovers in their Sunday walks!
The daisy and the buttercup –
For which the laughing children stoop
A hundred times throughout the day,
In their rude romping summer play –
So thickly now the pasture crowd,
In a gold and silver sheeted cloud,
As if the drops of April showers
Had woo'd the sun, and changed to flowers.
The brook resumes her summer dresses,
Purling 'neath grass and water-cresses,
And mint and flagleaf, swording high
Their blooms to the unheeding eye,
And taper, bow-bent, hanging rushes,

And horsetail, children's bottle-brushes;
The summer tracks about its brink
Are fresh again where cattle drink;
And on its sunny bank the swain
Stretches his idle length again;
While all that lives enjoys the birth
Of frolic summer's laughing mirth.

September

Harvest awakes the morning still,
And toil's rude groups the valleys fill;
Deserted is each cottage hearth
To all life, save the cricket's mirth;
Each burring wheel its sabbath meets,
Nor walks a gossip in the streets;
The bench beneath the eldern bough,
Lined o'er with grass, it is empty now,
Where blackbirds, caged from out the sun,
Would whistle while their mistress spun:
All haunt the thronged fields, to share
The harvest's lingering bounty there.

As yet, no meddling boys resort
About the streets in idle sport;
The butterfly enjoys its hour,
And flirts, unchased, from flower to flower;

The humming bees, which morning calls
From out the low hut's mortar walls,
And passing boy no more controls,
Fly undisturb'd about their holes;
The sparrows in glad chirpings meet,
Unpelted in the quiet street.
None but imprison'd children now
Are seen, where dames with angry brow
Threaten each younker to his seat,
Who, through the window, eyes the street,
Or from his hornbook turns away,
To mourn for liberty and play.

Yet loud are morning's early sounds;
The farm or cottage yard abounds
With creaking noise of opening gate,
And clanking pumps, where boys await
With idle motion, to supply
The thirst of cattle crowding nigh.
Upon the dovecote's mossy slates,
The pigeons coo around their mates;
And close beside the stable wall,
Where morning sunbeams earliest fall,
The basking hen, in playful rout,
Flaps the powdery dust about.
Within the barn-hole sits the cat
Watching to seize the thirsty rat,
Who oft at morn its dwelling leaves

To drink the moisture from the eaves;
The redbreast, with his nimble eye,
Dares scarcely stop to catch the fly,
That, tangled in the spider's snare,
Mourns in vain for freedom there.
The dog beside the threshold lies,
Mocking sleep, with half-shut eyes –
With head crouch'd down upon his feet,
Till strangers pass his sunny seat –
Then quick he pricks his ears to hark,
And bustles up to growl and bark;
While boys in fear stop short their song,
And sneak in startled speed along;
And beggar, creeping like a snail,
To make his hungry hopes prevail
O'er the warm heart of charity,
Leaves his lame halt and hastens by.

The maid afield now leaves the farm,
With dinner-basket on her arm,
Loitering unseen in narrow lane,
To be o'ertook by following swain,
Who, happy thus her truth to prove,
Carries the load and talks of love.
Soon as the dew is off the ground,
Rumbling like distant thunder round,
The wagons haste the corn to load,
And hurry down the dusty road;

While driving boy with eager eye
Watches the church clock passing by –
Whose gilt hands glitter in the sun –
To see how far the hours have run;
Right happy, in the breathless day,
To see time wearing fast away.
But now and then a sudden shower
Will bring to toil a resting hour;
Then, under sheltering shocks, a crowd
Of merry voices mingle loud,
Draining, with leisure's laughing eye,
Each welcome, bubbling bottle dry;
Till peeping suns dry up the rain,
Then off they start to toil again.

    Anon the fields are getting clear,
And glad sounds hum in labour's ear;
When children halloo, 'Here they come!'
And run to meet the Harvest Home,
Covered with boughs, and thronged with boys,
Who mingle loud a merry noise,
And, when they meet the stack-thronged yard
Cross-buns and pence their shouts reward.
Then comes the harvest-supper night,
Which rustics welcome with delight;
When merry game and tiresome tale,
And songs, increasing with the ale,
Their mingled uproar interpose,

To crown the harvest's happy close;
While Mirth, that at the scene abides,
Laughs, till she almost cracks her sides.

Now harvest's busy hum declines,
And labour half its help resigns.
Boys, glad at heart, to play return;
The shepherds to their peace sojourn,
Rush-bosom'd solitudes among,
Which busy toil disturb'd so long.
The gossip, happy all is o'er,
Visits again her neighbour's door,
On scandal's idle tales to dwell,
Which harvest had no time to tell;
And free from all its sultry strife,
Enjoys once more her idle life.
A few, whom waning toil reprieves,
Thread the forest's sea of leaves,
Where the pheasant loves to hide,
And the darkest glooms abide,
Beneath the old oaks moss'd and grey,
Whose shadows seem as old as they;
Where time hath many seasons won,
Since aught beneath them saw the sun;
Within these brambly solitudes,
The ragged, noisy boy intrudes,
To gather nuts, that, ripe and brown,
As soon as shook will patter down.

Thus harvest ends its busy reign,
And leaves the fields their peace again,
Where autumn's shadows idly muse
And tinge the trees in many hues:
Amid whose scenes I'm fain to dwell,
And sing of what I love so well.
But hollow winds, and tumbling floods,
And humming showers, and moaning woods,
All startle into sadden strife,
And wake a mighty lay to life,
Making, amid their strains divine,
Unheard a song so mean as mine.

December

Glad Christmas comes, and every hearth
   Makes room to give him welcome now,
E'en want will dry its tears in mirth,
   And crown him with a holly bough;
Though tramping 'neath a winter sky,
   O'er snowy paths and rimy stiles,
The housewife sets her spinning by
   To bid him welcome with her smiles.

Each house is swept the day before,
   And windows stuck with evergreens,
The snow is besom'd from the door,

And comfort crowns the cottage scenes.
Gilt holly, with its thorny pricks,
    And yew and box, with berries small,
These deck the unused candlesticks,
    And pictures hanging by the wall.

Neighbours resume their annual cheer,
    Wishing, with smiles and spirits high,
Glad Christmas and a happy year
    To every morning passer-by;
Milkmaids their Christmas journeys go,
    Accompanied with favour'd swain;
And children pace the crumping snow,
    To taste their granny's cake again.

The shepherd, now no more afraid,
    Since custom doth the chance bestow,
Starts up to kiss the giggling maid
    Beneath the branch of misletoe
That 'neath each cottage beam is seen,
    With pearl-like berries shining gay;
The shadow still of what hath been,
    Which fashion yearly fades away.

The singing waits, a merry throng,
    At early morn, with simple skill,
Yet imitate the angels' song,
    And chant their Christmas ditty still;

And, mid the storm that dies and swells
    By fits, in hummings softly steals
The music of the village bells,
    Ringing round their merry peals.

When this is past, a merry crew,
    Bedeck'd in masks and ribbons gay,
The 'Morris-dance,' their sports renew,
    And act their winter evening play.
The clown turn'd king, for penny-praise,
    Storms with the actor's strut and swell;
And Harlequin, a laugh to raise,
    Wears his hunchback and tinkling bell.

And oft for pence and spicy ale,
    With winter nosegays pinn'd before,
The wassail-singer tells her tale,
    And drawls her Christmas carols o'er.
While prentice boy, with ruddy face,
    And rime-bepowder'd, dancing locks,
From door to door with happy pace,
    Runs round to claim his 'Christmas box.'

The block upon the fire is put,
    To sanction custom's old desires;
And many a faggot's bands are cut,
    For the old farmers' Christmas fires;
Where loud-tongued Gladness joins the throng,

And Winter meets the warmth of May,
Till feeling soon the heat too strong,
  He rubs his shins, and draws away.

While snows the window-panes bedim,
  The fire curls up a sunny charm,
Where, creaming o'er the pitcher's rim,
  The flowering ale is set to warm;
Mirth, full of joy as summer bees,
  Sits there, its pleasures to impart,
And children, 'tween their parents' knees,
  Sing scraps of carols o'er by heart.

And some, to view the winter weathers,
  Climb up the window-seat with glee,
Likening the snow to falling feathers,
  In fancy's infant ecstasy;
Laughing, with superstitious love,
  O'er visions wild that youth supplies,
Of people pulling geese above,
  And keeping Christmas in the skies.

As tho' the homestead trees were drest,
  In lieu of snow, with dancing leaves,
As tho' the sun-dried martin's nest,
  Instead of ickles, hung the eaves,
The children hail the happy day –
  As if the snow were April's grass,

And pleas'd, as 'neath the warmth of May,
    Sport o'er the water froze to glass.

Thou day of happy sound and mirth,
    That long with childish memory stays,
How blest around the cottage hearth
    I met thee in my younger days!
Harping, with rapture's dreaming joys,
    On presents which thy coming found,
The welcome sight of little toys,
    The Christmas gift of cousins round:

The wooden horse with arching head,
    Drawn upon wheels around the room,
The gilded coach of gingerbread,
    And many-colour'd sugar-plum,
Gilt-cover'd books for pictures sought,
    Or stories childhood loves to tell,
With many an urgent promise bought,
    To get to-morrow's lesson well;

And many a thing, a minute's sport,
    Left broken on the sanded floor,
When we would leave our play, and court
    Our parents' promises for more.
Tho' manhood bids such raptures die,
    And throws such toys aside as vain,

Yet memory loves to turn her eye,
    And count past pleasures o'er again.

Around the glowing hearth at night,
    The harmless laugh and winter tale
Go round, while parting friends delight
    To toast each other o'er their ale;
The cotter oft with quiet zeal
    Will musing o'er his Bible lean;
While in the dark the lovers steal
    To kiss and toy behind the screen.

Old customs! Oh! I love the sound,
    However simple they may be:
Whate'er with time hath sanction found,
    Is welcome and is dear to me.
Pride grows above simplicity,
    And spurns them from her haughty mind,
And soon the poet's song will be
    The only refuge they can find.

Proposals For Building a Cottage

Beside a runnel build my shed,
    With stubbles cover'd o'er;
Let broad oaks o'er its chimney spread,
    And grass-plats grace the door.

The door may open with a string,
    So that it closes tight;
And locks would be a wanted thing,
    To keep out thieves at night.

A little garden, not too fine,
    Inclose with painted pales;
And woodbines, round the cot to twine,
    Pin to the wall with nails.

Let hazels grow, and spindling sedge,
    Bent bowering overhead;
Dig old man's beard from woodland hedge,
    To twine a summer shade.

Beside the threshold sods provide,
    And build a summer seat;
Plant sweetbrier bushes by its side,
    And flowers that blossom sweet.

I love the sparrows' ways to watch
    Upon the cotters' sheds,
So here and there pull out the thatch,
    That they may hide their heads.

And as the sweeping swallows stop
    Their flights along the green,
Leave holes within the chimney-top
    To paste their nest between.

Stick shelves and cupboards round the hut,
    In all the holes and nooks;
Nor in the corner fail to put
    A cupboard for the books.

Along the floor some sand I'll sift,
    To make it fit to live in;
And then I'll thank ye for the gift,
    As something worth the giving.

Love's Riddle

'Unriddle this riddle, my own Jenny love,
    Unriddle this riddle for me,
And if ye unriddle the riddle aright,
    A kiss your prize shall be,
And if ye riddle the riddle all wrong,
    Ye'll treble the debt to me:

'I'll give thee an apple without any core;
I'll give thee a cherry where stones never be;
I'll give thee a palace without any door,
And thou shall unlock it without any key;
I'll give thee a fortune that kings cannot give,
    Nor any one take from thee.'

'How can there be apples without any core?
How can there be cherries where stone never be?
How can there be houses without any door?
Or doors I may open without any key?
How canst thou give fortunes that kings cannot give,
     When thou art no richer than me?'

'My head is the apple without any core;
In cherries in blossom no stones ever be;
My mind is love's palace without any door,
Which thou canst unlock, love, without any key.
My heart is the wealth, love, that kings cannot give,
     Nor any one take it from thee.

'So there are love's riddles, my own Jenny love,
     Ye cannot unriddle to me,
And for one kiss you've so easily lost
     I'll make ye give seven to me.
To kiss thee is sweet, but 'tis sweeter by far
     To be kissed, my dear Jenny, by thee.

'Come pay me the forfeit, my own Jenny love;
     Thy kisses and cheeks are akin,
And for thy three sweet ones I'll give thee a score
     On thy cheeks, and thy lips, and thy chin.'

She laughed while he gave them, as much as to say,
    ''Twere better to lose than to win.'

A Fine Old Ballad

Fare you well, my own true love,
And fare you well for a while;
And I will be sure to return back again
If I go ten thousand miles, my dear,
    If I go ten thousand miles.

Ten thousand mile's a long long way,
When from me you are gone;
You'll leave me here to lament and sigh
But never shall hear me moan, my dear,
    But never shall hear me moan.

To hear you moan I cannot bear,
Or cure you of your disease;
I shall be sure to return back again
When all your friends are pleased, my dear,
    When all your friends are pleased.

If my friends should never be pleased –
They're grown so lofty and high –

I will never prove false to the girl I love
Till the stars they fall from the sky, my love,
   Till the stars they fall from the sky.

Oh, if the stars never fall from the sky
Nor the rocks never melt in the sun,
I never will prove false to the girl I love
Till all these things are done, my dear,
   Till all these things are done.

Don't you see yon little turtle-dove
That sits on yonder tree,
Making a moan for the loss of her love
As I will do for thee, my dear,
   As I will do for thee?

The blackest crow that ever flies
Shall change his colour white,
And if ever I prove false to thee, my love,
The day shall turn to night, my dear,
   The day shall turn to night.

But if these things ne'er come to pass
So long as we both do live,
I ne'er will prove false, my love, to thee
Till we're both laid in one grave, my dear,
   Till we're both laid in one grave.

The Thrush's Nest

Within a thick and spreading hawthorn bush
    That overhung a mole-hill large and round,
I heard from morn to morn a merry thrush
    Sing hymns to sunrise, while I drank the sound
With joy; and, often an intruding guest,
    I watched her secret toils from day to day –
How true she warped the moss to form a nest,
    And modelled it within with wood and clay;
And by and by, like heath-bells gilt with dew,
    There lay her shining eggs, as bright as flowers,
Ink-spotted over shells of greeny blue;
    And there I witnessed, in the sunny hours,
A brood of nature's minstrels chirp and fly,
Glad as that sunshine and the laughing sky.

Remembrances

Summer's pleasures they are gone like to visions every one,
And the cloudy days of autumn and winter cometh on.
I tried to call them back, but unbidden they are gone
Far away from heart and eye and for ever far away.
Dear heart, and can it be that such raptures meet decay?
I thought them all eternal when by Langley Bush I lay,
I thought them joys eternal when I used to shout and play

On its bank at 'clink and bandy,' 'chock' and 'taw' and
   'ducking stone,'
Where silence sitteth now on the wild heath as her own
Like a ruin of the past all alone.

When I used to lie and sing by old Eastwell's boiling spring,
When I used to tie the willow boughs together for a swing,
And fish with crooked pins and thread and never catch a
   thing,
With heart just like a feather, now as heavy as a stone;
When beneath old Lea Close Oak I the bottom branches
   broke
To make our harvest cart like so many working folk,
And then to cut a straw at the brook to have a soak.
Oh, I never dreamed of parting or that trouble had a sting,
Or that pleasures like a flock of birds would ever take to
   wing,
Leaving nothing but a little naked spring.

When jumping time away on old Crossberry Way,
And eating haws like sugarplums ere they had lost the may,
And skipping like a leveret before the peep of day
On the roly-poly up and downs of pleasant Swordy Well,
When in Round Oak's narrow lane as the south got black
   again
We sought the hollow ash that was shelter from the rain,
With our pockets full of peas we had stolen from the grain;
How delicious was the dinner-time on such a showery day! 43

Oh, words are poor receipts for what time hath stole away,
The ancient pulpit trees and the play.

When for school o'er Little Field with its brook and wooden
    brig,
Where I swaggered like a man though I was not half so big,
While I held my little plough though 'twas but a willow
    twig,
And drove my team along made of nothing but a name,
'Gee hep' and 'hoit' and 'woi' – oh, I never call to mind
These pleasant names of places but I leave a sigh behind,
While I see the little mouldiwarps hang sweeing to the wind
On the only aged willow that in all the field remains,
And nature hides her face while they're sweeing in their
    chains
And in a silent murmuring complains.

Here was commons for their hills, where they seek for
    freedom still,
Though every common's gone and though traps are set to
    kill
The little homeless miners – oh, it turns my bosom chill
When I think of old Sneap Green, Puddock's Nook and
    Hilly Snow,
Where bramble bushes grew and the daisy gemmed in dew
And the hills of silken grass like to cushions to the view,
Where we threw the pismire crumbs when we'd nothing
    else to do,
All levelled like a desert by the never-weary plough,

All vanished like the sun where that cloud is passing now
And settled here for ever on its brow.

Oh, I never thought that joys would run away from boys,
Or that boys would change their minds and forsake such
    summer joys;
But alack, I never dreamed that the world had other boys
To petrify first feeling like the fable into stone,
Till I found the pleasure past and a winter come at last,
Then the fields were sudden bare and the sky got overcast,
And boyhood's pleasing haunts, like a blossom in the blast,
Was shrivelled to a withered weed and trampled down and
    done,
Till vanished was the morning spring and set the summer
    sun,
And winter fought her battle strife and won.

By Langley Bush I roam, but the bush hath left its hill,
On Cowper Green I stray, 'tis a desert strange and chill,
And the spreading Lea Close Oak, ere decay had penned its
    will,
To the axe of the spoiler and self-interest fell a prey,
And Crossberry Way and old Round Oak's narrow lane
With its hollow trees like pulpits I shall never see again,
Enclosure like a Buonaparte let not a thing remain,
It levelled every bush and tree and levelled every hill
And hung the moles for traitors – though the brook is
    running still
It runs a naked stream, cold and chill.

Oh, had I known as then joy had left the paths of men,
I had watched her night and day, be sure, and never slept
    agen,
And when she turned to go, oh, I'd caught her mantle then,
And wooed her like a lover by my lonely side to stay;
Ay, knelt and worshipped on, as love in beauty's bower,
And clung upon her smiles as a bee upon a flower,
And gave her heart my posies, all cropt in a sunny hour,
As keepsakes and pledges all to never fade away;
But love never heeded to treasure up the may,
So it went the common road to decay.

Badger

When midnight comes a host of dogs and men
Go out and track the badger to his den,
And put a sack within the hole, and lie
Till the old grunting badger passes by.
He comes and hears – they let the strongest loose.
The old fox hears the noise and drops the goose.
The poacher shoots and hurries from the cry,
And the old hare half wounded buzzes by.
They get a forked stick to bear him down
And clap the dogs and take him to the town,
And bait him all the day with many dogs,
And laugh and shout and fright the scampering hogs.
He runs along and bites at all he meets:
They shout and hollo down the noisy streets.

He turns about to face the loud uproar
And drives the rebels to their very door.
The frequent stone is hurled where'er they go;
When badgers fight, then every one's a foe.
The dogs are clapt and urged to join the fray;
The badger turns and drives them all away.
Though scarcely half as big, demure and small,
He fights with dogs for hours and beats them all.
The heavy mastiff, savage in the fray,
Lies down and licks his feet and turns away.
The bulldog knows his match and waxes cold,
The badger grins and never leaves his hold.
He drives the crowd and follows at their heels
And bites them through – the drunkard swears and reels.

The frighted women take the boys away,
The blackguard laughs and hurries on the fray.
He tries to reach the woods, an awkward race,
But sticks and cudgels quickly stop the chase.
He turns agen and drives the noisy crowd
And beats the many dogs in noises loud.
He drives away and beats them every one,
And then they loose them all and set them on.
He falls as dead and kicked by boys and men,
Then starts and grins and drives the crowd agen;
Till kicked and torn and beaten out he lies
And leaves his hold and cackles, groans, and dies.

Child Harold: Two Songs

I

Say what is Love – to live in vain
To live & die & live again

Say what is Love – is it to be
In prison still & still be free

Or seem as free – alone & prove
The hopeless hopes of real Love

Does real Love on earth exist
Tis like a sunbeam on the mist

That fades & nowhere will remain
& nowhere is oertook again

Say what is Love – a blooming name
A rose leaf on the page of fame

That blooms then fades – to cheat no more
& is what nothing was before

Say what is Love – what e'er it be
It centres Mary still with thee

II

I've wandered many a weary mile
– Love in my heart was burning –
To seek a home in Marys smile

But cold is lifes sojourning
The cold ground was a feather-bed
Truth never acts contrary
I had no home above my head
My home was love & Mary

I had no home in early youth
When my first love was thwarted
But if her heart still beats with truth
We'll never more be parted
& changing as her love may be
My own shall never vary
Nor night nor day I'm never free
But sigh for abscent Mary

Nor night nor day nor sun nor shade
Week month nor rolling year
Repairs the breach wronged love hath made
There madness – misery here
Lifes lease was lengthened by her smiles
– Are truth & love contrary
No ray of hope my fate beguiles –
I've lost love home & Mary

Love Lies Beyond The Tomb

Love lies beyond
The tomb, the earth, which fades like dew!
    I love the fond,
The faithful, and the true.

Love lives in sleep,
The happiness of healthy dreams:
　　Eve's dews may weep,
But love delightful seems.

'Tis seen in flowers,
And in the even's pearly dew;
　　On earth's green hours,
And in the heaven's eternal blue.

'Tis heard in spring
When light and sunbeams, warm and kind,
　　On angel's wing
Bring love and music to the mind.

And where is voice,
So young, so beautifully sweet
　　As nature's choice,
When spring and lovers meet?

Love lies beyond
The tomb, the earth, the flowers, and dew.
　　I love the fond,
The faithful, young, and true.

An Invite, to Eternity

Wilt thou go with me, sweet maid,
Say, maiden, wilt thou go with me
Through the valley-depths of shade,
Of night and dark obscurity;
Where the path has lost its way,
Where the sun forgets the day,
Where there's nor life nor light to see,
Sweet maiden, wilt thou go with me?

Where stones will turn to flooding steams,
Where plains will rise like ocean waves,
Where life will fade like visioned dreams
And mountains darken into caves,
Say, maiden, wilt thou go with me
Through this sad non-identity,
Where parents live and are forgot,
And sisters live and know us not?

Say, maiden, wilt thou go with me
In this strange death of life to be,
To live in death and be the same,
Without this life or home or name,
At once to be and not to be –
That was and is not – yet to see
Things pass like shadows, and the sky
Above, below, around us lie?

The land of shadows wilt thou trace,
And look – nor know each other's face;
The present mixed with reason gone,
And past and present all as one?
Say, maiden, can thy life be led
To join the living with the dead?
Then trace thy footsteps on with me;
We're wed to one eternity.

I am

I am – yet what I am none cares or knows,
  My friends forsake me like a memory lost;
I am the self-consumer of my woes,
    They rise and vanish in oblivions host,
Like shadows in love – frenzied stifled throes
And yet I am, and live like vapours tost

Into the nothingness of scorn and noise,
  Into the living sea of waking dreams,
Where there is neither sense of life or joys,
    But the vast shipwreck of my life's esteems;
And e'en the dearest – that I love the best –
Are strange – nay, rather stranger than the rest.

I long for scenes where man has never trod,
    A place where woman never smiled or wept;

There to abide with my Creator, God,
    And sleep as I in childhood sweetly slept:
Untroubling and untroubled where I lie,
The grass below – above the vaulted sky.

A Vision

I lost the love of heaven above,
    I spurned the lust of earth below,
I felt the sweets of fancied love,
    And hell itself my only foe.

I lost earth's joys, but felt the glow
    Of heaven's flame abound in me,
Till loveliness and I did grow
    The bard of immortality.

I loved, but woman fell away;
    I hid me from her faded fame.
I snatched the sun's eternal ray
    And wrote till earth was but a name.

In every language upon earth,
    On every shore, o'er every sea,

I gave my name immortal birth
   And kept my spirit with the free.

August 2nd, 1844

Sonnet

Enough of misery keeps my heart alive
To make it feel more mental agony:
Till even life itself becomes all pain,
And bondage more than hell to keep alive;
And still I live, nor murmur nor complain,
Save that the bonds which hold me may make free
My lonely solitude and give me rest,
When every foe hath ceased to trouble me
On the soft throbbing of a woman's breast;
Where love and truth and feeling live confest.
The little cottage with those bonds of joy
My family – life's blood within my breast
Is not more dear than is each girl and boy
Which time matures and nothing can destroy.

Love's Story

I do not love thee
So I'll not deceive thee.
I do not love thee,
Yet I'm loth to leave thee.

I do not love thee
Yet joy's very essence
Comes with thy footstep,
Is complete in thy presence.

I do not love thee
Yet when gone, I sigh
And think about thee
Till the stars all die

I do not love thee
Yet thy bright black eyes
Bring to my heart's soul
Heaven and paradise

I do not love thee
Yet thy handsome ways
Bring me in absence
Almost hopeless days

I cannot hate thee
Yet my love seems debtor
To love thee more
So hating, love thee better.

First Love

I ne'er was struck before that hour
　　With love so sudden and so sweet.
Her face it bloomed like a sweet flower
　　And stole my heart away complete.
My face turned pale as deadly pale,
　　My legs refused to walk away,
And when she looked 'what could I ail?'
　　My life and all seemed turned to clay.

And then my blood rushed to my face
　　And took my eyesight quite away.
The trees and bushes round the place
　　Seemed midnight at noonday.
I could not see a single thing,
　　Words from my eyes did start;
They spoke as chords do from the string
　　And blood burnt round my heart.

Are flowers the winter's choice?
　　Is love's bed always snow?
She seemed to hear my silent voice
　　Not love's appeals to know.
I never saw so sweet a face
　　As that I stood before:
My heart has left its dwelling-place
　　And can return no more.

Song

I Hid My Love

I hid my love when young while I
Couldn't bear the buzzing of a fly;
I hid my love to my despite
Till I could not bear to look at light:
I dare not gaze upon her face
But left her memory in each place;
Where'er I saw a wild flower lie
I kissed and bade my love good-bye.

I met her in the greenest dells,
Where dewdrops pearl the wood bluebells;
The lost breeze kissed her bright blue eye,
The bee kissed and went singing by,
A sunbeam found a passage there,
A gold chain round her neck so fair;
As secret as the wild bee's song
She lay there all the summer long.

I hid my love in field and town
Till e'en the breeze would knock me down;
The Bees seemed singing ballads o'er,
The flyes buzz turned a Lion's roar;
And even silence found a tongue,
To haunt me all the summer long;
The riddle nature could not prove
Was nothing else but secret love.

Born Upon An Angel's Breast

In crime and enmity they lie
Who sin and tell us love can die,
Who say to us in slander's breath
That love belongs to sin and death.
From Heaven it came on Angel's wing
To bloom on earth, Eternal spring;
In falsehood's enmity they lie
Who sin and tell us love can die.

'Twas born upon an angel's breast.
The softest dreams, the sweetest rest,
The brightest sun, the bluest sky,
Are love's own home and canopy.
The thought that cheers this heart of mine
Is that of Love – Love so divine,
They sin who say in slander's breath
That love belongs to sin and death.

The sweetest voice that lips contain,
The sweetest thought that leaves the brain,
The sweetest feeling of the heart –
There's pleasure even in its smart.
The scent of Rose and Cinnamon
Is not like Love remembered on;
In falsehood's enmity they lie
Who sin and tell us love can die.

A Note on John Clare

John Clare (1793–1864), the English poet, was born at Helpstone, Northamptonshire. The son of a poor labourer, he was known as a 'peasant poet'. At the age of seven he worked on a farm, and later as an under-gardener, but in 1812 he ran away and joined the militia. For a time he lived with gypsies, then worked as a burner on a lime kiln but was dismissed and forced to seek for parish relief.

Clare enjoyed listening to and learning old ballads, and when very young scribbled verses of his own. His inspiration came from Thomson's *Seasons*, and his poems deal with country life and farm scenes, revealing keen powers of observation and a love of nature. *Poems Descriptive of Rural Life and Scenery*, 1820, was very well received, and was followed in 1821 by *The Village Minstrel*. On visiting London, Clare was helped by men of influence and wealth. He was encouraged by other literary figures, though not always well advised, and became a friend of Charles Lamb. He married in 1820 and, with a family of seven children, was always poor, though he was given labouring work from time to time. The *Shepherd's Calendar*, 1827, and *The Rural Muse*, 1835, were less successful than his earlier works, but the latter brought him £40 and was praised by Christopher North.

Eventually his health broke down; he suffered from mental delusions and spent the last 23 years of his life in the Northamptonshire asylum, still writing lyrical poetry, including his last poem, 'I am: yet what I am who cares or knows?'. His close observation and love of nature resulted in a use of fresh and penetrating imagery, and some of his descriptive pieces are among the best in the English language.